❧ A HISTORY ❧ OF FORT SCREVEN GEORGIA

TYBEE ISLAND'S MILITARY HERITAGE

COMPILED BY
JAMES E. GROOVER
AND
JAMES MACK ADAMS

WRITTEN BY
JAMES MACK ADAMS

❧ ❧

Tybee Island Historical Society
Tybee Island, Georgia
2002

Library of Congress Catalog Card Number: 94-79902
ISBN 0-9644723-0-9
Printed in the United States of America.

Book Design and Layout By Wayman H. Benton.

All photographs and illustrations, unless otherwise noted, are furnished courtesy of the Tybee Island Historical Society and James E. Groover.

Cover photo, "Flowered Fortress," by Joseph Shields.

Typesetting and publication arrangements by
    The Reprint Company, Publishers
    P.O. Box 5401
    Spartanburg, South Carolina 29304

Dedication

To the men of the Eighth Infantry Regiment, the Coast Artillery Companies, the Port Construction and Repair Groups, and the other military units that served at Fort Screven, and to the civilian men and women who took part in the fort's construction, operation and maintenance.

Contents

❧ A HISTORY ❧
OF
FORT SCREVEN
GEORGIA

Acknowledgements

The author is particularly indebted to James E. "Popeye" Groover, who was the inspiration for this project and who supplied the major portion of the research that made this book possible. Groover served with the Eighth Infantry Regiment at Fort Screven and for many years has been president of the Fort Screven Association, a group of Eighth Infantry veterans who have their yearly reunion at Tybee Island.

A very special thanks to fellow writers Jefferson Dukes, Miriam Reid Shaffer and Wayman Benton for their unbiased critique of the manuscript and their many constructive suggestions.

Much appreciation to the other readers of the manuscript:

Colonel, United States Army (Ret.) Donald M. Harris for his welcomed historical input.

Colonel, United States Army (Ret.) James P. Locklear, who grew up at Fort Screven, where his father served as hospital Sergeant-Major.

Cullen Chambers, Director of the Tybee Island Historical Society, for opening the Society's files to the author.

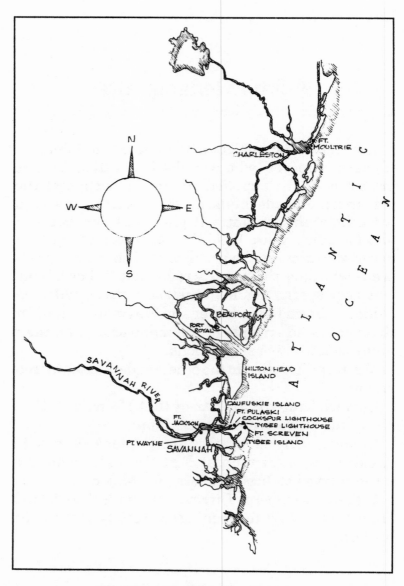

Sketch map of Southeast coast.
Courtesy of Michael Griffith

❧ Prologue ❧

Tybee's Early History

Although Tybee Island is but a tiny piece of land, being only 2 1/2 miles long and 2/3 of a mile wide, its strategic location at the mouth of the Savannah River assigned it an important role in the settling of the New World. History books detail fascinating accounts of Tybee's contributions to the birth and history of Georgia, one of the 13 original colonies. Legends speak of the island as a destination for early explorers searching for the "Fountain of Youth" and as a stopover for pirates, including the infamous Blackbeard. Flags of five nations have flown over Tybee Island— Spain, France, England, The Confederate States of America and The United States of America.

Three theories compete to explain Tybee's name. One belief, the most widely accepted, is that the island was named by the Euchee Indians who came to the coast to fish. Tybee was the Euchee word for salt. Perhaps those native Americans chose this name because of the saltwater surrounding the island. Another theory is that the island was named for the Choctaw Indian Chief, Iti Ubi. A third school of thought is that the name Tybee is a derivative of the word tabby, a crushed oyster shell building material popular with early settlers along the Georgia coast.

The earliest record of European influence on Tybee

1

was the arrival of the Spanish in the early 1500's. Tybee then became a part of the Spanish claims in the new world. The stretch of coastline from St. Augustine, Florida northward to Port Royal, South Carolina became known as La Florida, or Bimini.

During this period of Spanish influence, the island was occasionally visited by Spanish explorers. Lucas Vazques de Ayllon sailed from the Antilles with a dream of establishing a European colony on the Atlantic seaboard. He did visit Tybee, but historians believe that his doomed colony was situated further south, perhaps in what is now McIntosh County. When Hernando DeSoto visited Tybee in 1540, he found a rosary and a knife that he believed had belonged to the Ayllon party.

Another Spaniard, Captain Francisco de Ecija, is credited with the first known written description of Tybee Island. In his writings, he referred to Tybee Roads, at the mouth of the Savannah River, as the Bay of Shoals.

Tybee played a small part in the drama of Ponce de Leon's search for the legendary "Fountain of Youth." The bark of the sassafras tree was thought by some to be the closest known thing to this mystical restorer of youth. In 1605, sailors from a French vessel landed on the Island to trade with the Indians and to search for sassafras bark. Hearing about this interest in Tybee sassafras, Captain Ecija and his men attacked and captured the French ship.

In 1733, when General James Edward Oglethorpe sailed into the Savannah River to establish the English colony of Georgia and the city of Savannah, he immediately recognized the strategic importance of Tybee Island. In a letter to his trustees in England, Oglethorpe said, "The river is pretty wide, the water fresh, and from the key of the town you can see its whole course to the sea, with the island of Tybee, which forms the mouth of the river."

Recognizing that the survival of his new colony depended on the safe passage of settlers and supplies into the Savannah River, Oglethorpe ordered Noble Jones of Wormsloe Plantation to direct the construction of a lighthouse on Tybee Island. When in 1736, Jones completed his 90-foot tower, some people declared it the tallest structure of its kind in America. Throughout its long history, Tybee's lighthouse has been destroyed by storms and by acts of war. It has been rebuilt, remodeled and moved back from the raging seas. The lighthouse was constructed on its present site in 1773. This is the structure around which Fort Screven was built.

John Wesley, the father of Methodism, visited the new colony in February of 1736. He said his first prayer on the American continent at Cockspur Island, which is about 2 miles from Tybee. Oglethorpe gave the island its first name, Peeper Island. Pilots entering the Savannah River could see the small island "peeping" around the north shoulder of Tybee. The name was changed to Cockspur Island sometime in the 1730's.

That Wesley was fascinated with Tybee's beauty and its pleasing climate is attested by an article in his journal: "We cast anchor near Tybee Island, where groves of pines running along the shore made an agreeable prospect, showing as it were, the bloom of Spring in the depth of Winter."

In 1749 an act was passed that permitted the importation of slaves to Georgia. This led to the establishment on Tybee of a hospital, called a Lazaretto, for the quarantine and treatment of contagious diseases. Lazaretto is a now obsolete Italian word meaning pest house.

The colony's authorities boarded all vessels arriving at the mouth of the Savannah River; passengers and crew were checked for signs of disease. If they discovered a contagious disease, they forbad the ship to enter the port for a period of forty days, hence the word *quarantine*. Ill persons were removed to the hospital and remained there until they were determined to be free of the disease, or had died. Those who died were buried on the site in unmarked graves.

Just prior to the opening shot of the American Revolution, the British Governor of Georgia, fearing for his life, sought refuge at Tybee. He and other officials boarded a British man-of-war anchored off Cockspur Island. From this off-shore refuge the governor and his party made occasional pleasure trips to Tybee. When the governor's whereabouts became known, a group of patriots came from Savannah to Tybee in search of him. While the patriots were burning the island's few houses, the governor sailed for England.

Two years passed before Tybee again became involved in the Revolution. In December of 1778 a British invasion force appeared off Tybee Island. Savannah's defense was a fiasco and the city fell almost without a shot.

In 1779 a combined force of French and Americans under the command of Comte Jean Baptiste Charles Henri Hector d'Estaing came ashore to storm Fort Tybee, Which stood where Fort Screven now stands. The attackers found the fort empty.

The French and American force then laid siege to Savannah in an unsuccessful attempt to retake the city from the British. Historians classify the American and French assault on the British defenses as one of the bloodiest battles of the American Revolution, second only to Bunker Hill. Killed in this battle was Count Casmir Pulaski, a Polish nobleman who fought for the American cause. Fort Pulaski on Cockspur Island was named in his honor.

The Americans and the British confronted each other again in the War of 1812. Savannah and Tybee prepared for another British assault which never came. This preparation included an elaborate system of signals to give the militiamen charged with defending Savannah warning of an impending British attack. The Tybee lighthouse keeper was to signal watchers at Fort Jackson of the enemy's approach. The signal was to then be relayed to Fort Wayne on the edge of Savannah and from there to the watchman stationed in the steeple of the old Cotton Exchange.

At sometime between 1812 and 1815, the federal government constructed a lookout tower and fort on the beach near the lighthouse. The structure was known as the Martello Tower and was patterned after similar fortifications built on the south and east coasts of England after 1800. Master builder Isaiah Davenport of Savannah is believed to have supervised the construction of the tower. Other such towers, some quite different in style, were built in several states, including Louisiana, Florida, South Carolina and New Hampshire. Tybee's Martello Tower survived for nearly 100 years before it was destroyed to clear the field of fire for Fort Screven's guns.

During the Pre-Civil War plantation era, the Martello Tower served as a site for the settling of affairs of honor. Because dueling was outlawed in South Carolina, many southern gentlemen crossed the river to Tybee to settle their disputes. The blood of many Carolinians was shed in the sand surrounding the Martello Tower and the lighthouse.

The Martello Tower eventually was used as a post office and became the home of Elizabeth Lockwood Wortham, the first postmistress, when the town was incorporated under the name of Savannah Beach in 1887.

A few years after the end of the War of 1812, Tybee again played a role in an historic event. In May, 1819

The Martello Tower, 1860's
Thomas Gamble Collection

Elizabeth Wortham and one of her children, 1888.

the *Savannah*, the first steamship to cross the Atlantic, made its maiden voyage from Savannah to Tybee. Included among its passengers was President James Monroe, who was visiting friends in Savannah. The *Savannah* passed Tybee once more a few days later on its historic voyage to Liverpool, England.

The history of Tybee Island makes clear the fact that this small barrier island has for centuries been recognized as a militarily strategic location. Union army commanders recognized this when they set up their artillery and bombarded Fort Pulaski during America's Civil War. Tybee's strategic importance was later affirmed when big guns were mounted atop

Fort Screven's batteries. Adding to Fort Screven's historic importance is the fact that the fort joins the other Savannah River forts, Jackson and Pulaski, in illustrating the progression of military fort architecture throughout over 100 years of American history.

✦ 1 ✦

The War Between The States

In the mid-19th century, Tybee Island became an unwilling participant in what historians have called the bloodiest war in American history—the American Civil War. Its strategic location at the mouth of a major river leading into a major southern port, again made Tybee a prize for both sides. During the conflict, the small island played host, at different times, to both Federal and Confederate occupiers.

The smoldering fires of southern discontent with certain policies of the Federal government began to blaze anew after the election of President Abraham Lincoln in November, 1860. Approximately one month and a half later, December 20, 1860, South Carolina seceded from the Union. In a short time, Federal forces occupied Fort Sumter in Charleston harbor.

When news of the Federal garrisoning of Fort Sumter reached Savannah, the immediate fear among the city's officials was that the harbor of Savannah could suffer the same fate. If the Federals were allowed to occupy Fort Jackson and Fort Pulaski, which were river fortifications located between Tybee and Savannah, the Port of Savannah would be closed to all but Federally approved traffic.

Seeing a need for immediate action, Georgia Governor Joseph E. Brown ordered Georgia Militia forces to occupy Forts Jackson and Pulaski. On January 3, 1861, in a torrential rain, with flags flying and citizens cheering, the 1st Volunteer Regiment of Georgia, under the command of Colonel Alexander Lawton, marched to the pier at the end of West Broad Street in Savannah (now Martin Luther King, Jr. Boulevard) where they boarded the *Ida*, a commandeered federal side-wheeler. Arriving at Fort Pulaski, they took possession and raised the Georgia flag. Two weeks later, the state of Georgia followed the lead of its neighboring state of South Carolina and left the Union.

The offensive strategy of Federal military commanders was to blockade southern ports and capture seacoast fortifications. This would effectively seal southern ports and deny the Confederacy imports from Europe. Because the states that composed the Confederate States of America had primarily agrarian economies, this would cripple their war effort.

The Confederate strategy was by necessity defensive and was based on certain presumptions. Many Southern leaders were convinced that the war would not last over six months. The barrier islands, to include Tybee, would be the first line of defense against a Federal invasion from the sea. If the coastline was blockaded, some shipping could use the intercoastal waterway which is made up of numerous rivers, creeks and marshes.

Fort Pulaski would serve as the northern anchor of coastal defenses and Fort Clinch (Fernandina) would be the southern anchor. Many earthen or sand batteries would be dispersed between these two installations.

Confederate troops from Fort Pulaski boarded the *Ida* and occupied Tybee Island in the summer of 1861. Among the troops were elements of the Ist Georgia

Regulars who landed near the Martello Tower and set up their tents in an open area about 300 yards from the tower. Because there was no wharf, the Confederates had to wade ashore.

Sergeant William H. Andrews of Company M, Ist Georgia Regulars kept a journal in which he recorded his impressions and experiences throughout the war. In his journal, annotated and published by Longstreet Press under the title "Footprints of a Regiment," Andrews recorded some of his experiences during his tour of duty on Tybee.

It is evident from his writings that Andrews and his compatriots were not at all satisfied with their coast duty. He complained of the boredom and the isolation from the outside world. He suggested that the good behavior of the troops was attributable to the fact that they could not get off the island to get any whiskey. He stated that the troops were anxious to be sent to the front, preferring an active campaign to staying at Tybee where they were suffering from the heat and were being "ate up" by sand flies and mosquitoes.

Andrews wrote about being assigned guard duty at the top of the Tybee Lighthouse. His comments are not unlike some that are heard today from visitors to the lighthouse. He wrote, "One night it fell to my lot to be stationed on top of the lighthouse. It is octagon shaped, the stairs being on the inside. And how weak my knees got before I reached the top. It seemed as though I would never get there, but did at last."

Not long after the start of the Civil War, the numeric superiority of the Union navy became apparent. On November 7, 1861, a Federal naval task force of 40,000 troops captured and occupied Hilton Head Island, South Carolina, within sight of the Confederate troops on Tybee.

These and other developments caused a shift in

Southern defensive strategy. The lower Georgia coast (Darien and Brunswick) was deemed indefensible, and troops and guns were moved to bolster the defenses around Savannah. General Robert E. Lee also ordered the barrier islands abandoned and their troops concentrated along Savannah's defensive lines. Tybee Island was abandoned on November 10, 1861. Within a month, Federal forces from Hilton Head Island occupied Tybee. They established their headquarters near the lighthouse and Martello Tower.

During the brief interval when the island was not occupied by a military force, scouting parties of Federal troops from Hilton Head and Confederate troops from Fort Pulaski visited Tybee. On one of their night patrols, the Confederates destroyed the top of the lighthouse, to deny its use to Federal naval forces. The Federals had the lighthouse back in operation in a very short time.

The next obstacle the Union forces had to overcome was Fort Pulaski, which stands on Cockspur Island just across the Savannah River channel from Tybee. Completed in 1847, this fortress took eighteen years to build at a cost of nearly one million dollars. It was "state of the art" military construction and considered by many to be impregnable. An estimated 25 million bricks were used to construct the fort's 7 1/2 foot thick walls. The fort was completely encircled by a 7 foot deep moat. A young Lieutenant named Robert E. Lee supervised the early work on the fort.

After much effort, Captain Quincy A. Gillmore, Chief Engineer of the Federal forces occupying Hilton Head Island, convinced his superiors that Fort Pulaski could be successfully bombarded from Tybee. Among their available artillery pieces were several new and powerful rifled cannons. Rifling in the barrels of these guns gave them greater range and accuracy compared to the earlier smooth bore cannons.

From February 21 to April 9, 1862, Captain Gillmore supervised the work of soldiers of the 46th New York Volunteers as they constructed eleven earthen batteries, a total of thirty-six guns, on the north end of Tybee Island near Lazaretto Creek. The batteries were named for important Union military and civilian leaders—Stanton, Grant, Lyon, Lincoln, Burnside, Sherman, Halleck, Scott, Sigel, McClellan and Totten. The troops did their work under cover of darkness. Tarps camouflaged the guns during the day.

The Confederate soldiers at Fort Pulaski were aware of the Union activity on the far shore but believed themselves safe behind their thick walls. On a recent inspection of coastal fortifications, General Robert E. Lee had told the fort's commander, Colonel Charles H. Olmstead, that the walls of the fort could not be breached from that distance. At that time, of course, neither Lee nor any other of the Confederate leaders knew of the new technology of rifled cannon.

Shortly after dawn on April 10, a small boat, sailing under a flag of truce, approached Fort Pulaski and demanded its surrender. Colonel Olmstead refused the demand by saying, "I am here to defend the fort, not to surrender it."

A few minutes after 8:00 a.m., orders were given to begin the bombardment. Shells from the Tybee batteries began to smash into the fort's wall. The shelling continued until nightfall and resumed at dawn the next morning.

The Confederate gunners at Fort Pulaski did return the fire of the Federal guns, but their smooth bore cannons could not reach the Federal batteries. By noon the wall along the southeast angle of the fort

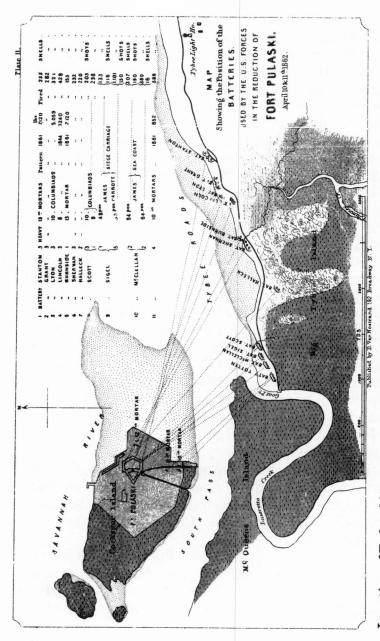

Location of Federal batteries on Tybee Island during the bombardment of Fort Pulaski (D. Van Norstrand and Fort Pulaski National Monument).

Union army soldiers at the Martello Tower, gun emplacements can be seen on the beach in the background.

began to crumble. With more direct hits, the breach in the wall widened until shells were passing through the gap and bouncing across the parade ground. The speeding projectiles began impacting dangerously close to the powder magazine, in the northwest corner.

Colonel Olmstead realized that he could no longer defend the fort and that if the powder magazine was hit a tremendous number of casualties would result. At mid-afternoon on the second day, after thirty hours of bombardment, Federal observers at the Tybee batteries saw the Confederate colors lowered and replaced by the white flag of surrender.

This was the only Civil War military engagement on Tybee. It proved to be an historically important one. The bombardment of Fort Pulaski helped to usher in a new era of military technology. The superiority of rifled over smooth bore cannon was proven beyond any doubt. Masonry and brick forts, once thought to be almost invincible, became obsolete. The designers and builders who later constructed Fort Screven were aware of this and fortified the outer walls of the batteries with dirt and sand. Fort Screven represented a new era in coastal fort construction.

❧ 2 ❧

Building Fort Screven

As the 19th Century came to a close, events happening just 90 miles off the Florida coast threatened to involve the United States in another armed conflict. In 1895, a Cuban revolt against Spanish rule resulted in a harsh retaliation by the Spanish government. Captured revolutionists were interned in squalid and overcrowded Cuban prisons resembling concentration camps. Thousands died from diseases directly caused by these conditions.

Due to Spain's colonialism in the Western Hemisphere, relations between that country and the United States had been strained for many years. The American press was instrumental in marshaling public opinion in support of the Cuban guerrillas. Some of the country's most prominent newspapers published accounts of atrocities against the Cuban people. Even though it was suspected by some that the accounts were exaggerated, there was a public outcry for U.S. intervention.

Economic considerations played a role in the call for Cuban independence. American investments in sugar and tobacco plantations, mines and railroads, as well as extensive trade, were threatened by the unstable situation.

In an 1896 speech before Congress, President Grover

Cleveland hinted that American intervention in the Cuban crisis might be necessary, The Congress was in general agreement with this policy. That same year, President Cleveland ordered the War Department to build or improve Atlantic coastal defenses to protect the U. S. coastline in the event of a war with Spain.

Twenty-four years earlier, in 1872, The U. S. Army Corps of Engineers had drawn up a plan for the construction of a fort on Tybee and had acquired the land on the north end of the island in 1875. Ten years later, in 1885, President Cleveland commissioned his Secretary of War, William C. Endicott, to make a study of the country's coastal defenses. After a year of traveling up and down the Pacific and Atlantic coasts, Endicott's committee submitted a 400 page report that called for the building of concrete and granite batteries, modification of some existing fortifications and the manufacture of new weapons. However, congressional appropriations to finance this massive building program were slow. Construction contracts were not let until the threat of war with Spain prompted action.

Early in 1897, the War Department published a map of actual or proposed Atlantic coast fortifications. Ranking high in priority was a proposed fortification to be constructed in the area adjacent to the lighthouse on Tybee Island, Georgia. According to documents, the fortification would house "the biggest cannon in the world".

The War Department later announced that the fort would be manned by the United States Army Coast Artillery. The troops would arrive as soon as a wharf was completed and buildings and gun emplacements constructed. The fort was first named Fort Tybee and later Fort Graham, for Brigadier General William

Montrose Graham, Commander of Atlantic coast defenses.

Within a short time, construction of the fort began. Most of the work on the buildings and gun emplacements was done by the Venable Construction Company under the supervision of the U. S. Army Corps of Engineers. Granite from north Georgia was used for the foundations of the gun batteries.

One of the engineers who helped guide the work on the fort's gun emplacements was Thomas Francis Lynch. In early 1897, Lynch was transferred from New Jersey to Savannah to supervise restoration work on Fort Pulaski. When that work was only half done, he was transferred to the new fortification on Tybee and resided at what later became Fort Screven for the remainder of his life. At the time of this writing his daughter, Nell (Lynch) Devine, still resides in the Fort Screven area and is considered one of the island's human treasures.

The first of the big guns being transported to the new fort never arrived. The schooner *Agnes D. Grace*, carrying four guns to Fort Graham, encountered a gale just off the Atlantic coast and sank. It was first thought that the guns could be salvaged since they were being transported on the ship's deck and therefore would not have sunk into the mud. However, efforts to locate the vessel proved fruitless and the search was finally abandoned. More guns were manufactured and eventually arrived at the fort.

On February 15, 1898, the American battleship *Maine*, anchored in the harbor of Havana to protect American interests, was sunk by a mysterious explosion. The explosion was later determined to be accidental. However, at the time, the American press and public judged the Spanish to be guilty of the deed and demanded action. On April 25, Congress declared war against Spain. The rallying cry became, "Remember The Maine."

Battery F of the First Coast Artillery, Company H of the Fifth Infantry and units of the Georgia militia were at Fort Graham on March 18, 1898 when it was officially established as a military post and renamed Fort Screven, for Brigadier General James Screven of the Georgia Militia, a hero of the American Revolution. In 1776, he was mortally wounded in a skirmish near Spencer's Hill in Liberty County. He died on the steps of the historic Midway Church, where he was taken for medical treatment.

Brigadier General James Screven
(Thomas Gamble Collection)

An act of heroism by a Fort Screven soldier took place during the fort's early days. On August 31, 1898, during a hurricane, the Italian Bark Noe was wrecked in Tybee Roads, putting the lives of the vessel's crew in jeopardy. Second Lieutenant Henry Sims Morgan and a crew of five volunteers launched a small boat and attempted to rescue the imperiled crew. Morgan and one companion drowned when the boat capsized. The 24-year-old Lieutenant was in charge of the fortification work at fort Screven.

A plaque dedicated to the memory of Lieutenant Morgan was placed at West Point by his classmates in 1903. In 1923, a duplicate of the plaque was mounted on a large granite stone and placed at Fort Screven. In 1950, six years after Fort Screven was inactivated, the monument was moved to nearby Fort Pulaski. In August 1994, this historic monument was returned to its rightful home in Fort Screven and placed in front of the Tybee Museum (Battery Garland).

Henry Sims Morgan Memorial

The seven gun batteries that composed Fort Screven were of a design that became known as the Endicott style of coastal fort construction, named after President Grover Cleveland's Secretary of War. By order of the President of the United States, each of the batteries was named for a member of the United States armed forces who had distinguished himself in one of the country's wars.

Battery Brumby was the first of the batteries to be completed and the only one that was in service during the short-lived Spanish American War. Construction of the battery was begun in April of 1897 under the supervision of Captain O. H. Carter of the Army Corps of Engineers. The battery was completed under the supervision of Captain Cassius E. Gillette in July of 1898. It was named for Lieutenant Thomas M. Brumby who served with the U. S. Navy in the Spanish American War. He was Admiral Dewey's Flag Lieutenant in the Battle of Manila Bay. Lieutenant Brumby died at Marietta, Georgia in 1900 from a disease contracted in military service. The battery had four 8-inch guns having a range of 10 miles. These were mounted on disappearing carriages. When a gun was fired, the recoil lowered it back and down below a protective parapet. The crew reloaded the gun in relative safety and mechanically raised it to fire again. The shells were stored in magazines inside the battery and were raised to the firing platform by an elevator. Crew members then used carts to wheel the shells to the guns. The operation of the battery required four officers and 157 men.

Battery Garland, one of Fort Screven's principal gun emplacements, was completed in March of 1899 and armed with one 12-inch rifled gun mounted on a non-disappearing carriage. Battery Garland was

8-Inch Gun mounted on disappearing carriage (Battery Brumby).

12-inch Gun (Battery Garland).

4.7-Inch Guns (Battery Backus).

12-Inch Mortar (Battery Habersham)

named for Brevet Brigadier General John Garland, a member of the U. S. Army in the war of 1812. He died in 1861 in New York City. This battery could be serviced by two officers and 47 men.

Battery Fenwick was armed with two 12-inch guns. It was named for Colonel John R. Fenwick, an artillery officer who served with distinction in the war of 1812 and died in 1842 at Marseilles, France.

Construction of Battery Backus began on April 27, 1898 and the first 6- inch rapid-fire gun was mounted on September 6 of that year. The gun was replaced in 1905 by a more modern 4.7-inch gun. Two additional gun emplacements were completed in 1900 and were armed with two more 4.7-inch guns. Battery Backus was named for Colonel Electus Backus who also served with the U. S, Army during the War of 1812. Backus died on June 7, of wounds received in the Battle of Sackett's Harbor, New York.

Battery Gantt was named to honor First Lieutenant Levi Gantt, who was killed in the battle of Chapultepec, Mexico in 1847. This battery was armed with two 3-inch rapid-fire guns which, along with the Battery Backus guns, guarded the submerged minefields at the mouth of the Savannah River. The battery was completed in February 1900, but the guns were not mounted until September 1903. One officer and twenty-five men were required to operate this battery.

Battery Habersham was named for Major Joseph Habersham, a member of the Continental Army during the Revolutionary War. Habersham served as Postmaster General of the United states from 1785 to 1801. He died in 1815 at Savannah, Georgia. This battery is said to have contained the most effective armament at Fort Screven. Eight 12-inch steel rifled mortars, arranged in three emplacements, fired 700 pound shells in a high arc to descend on the decks of enemy ships. The construction of Battery Habersham was started in December 1898, one month after the war with Spain ended. The guns were in place by June of 1900. The battery was served by seven officers and 219 enlisted men.

Battery Hambright on Cockspur Island

To provide additional protection to Savannah Harbor, the War Department constructed Battery Hambright on Cockspur Island, near Fort Pulaski. Work on Battery Hambright began on June 1, 1899. The battery had emplacements for two 3-inch rapid fire guns that could fire upon ships approaching Savannah by the north channel.

During the Spanish-American War this channel was protected by a submerged minefield that was controlled from Fort Pulaski. When a ship struck a buoy that was attached to each mine, an electrical signal alerted observers stationed in the mining casemate at Fort Pulaski. If the vessel was determined to be unfriendly, the observers could electrically detonate the mines.

As the 19th Century came to a close, the construction of fort facilities continued. In November of 1899, the troop strength at Fort Screven increased by 180 men with the arrival by train of Battery C, 2nd Coast Artillery. In that same month, a week-long tent revival was held in the Town of Savannah Beach (Tybee). News reports of the event stated that a third of those in attendance were soldiers from Fort Screven.

❧ 3 ☙

Early 1900's And World War I

In the short-lived war with Spain, Fort Screven's big guns were never "fired in anger." However, the gun crews kept their gunnery skills sharpened through drills and target practice. By the turn of the century, the guns were being fired on a regular schedule.

Fort Screven continued to grow and change during the interval between 1900 and World War I. United States military planners felt that there was a need to keep the nation's coastal fortifications in a state of readiness. One reason for this policy was the possible threat posed by a world-wide expansion of German submarine activity. Also, the Monroe Doctrine claimed that the United States possessed the right to intervene in Latin-American affairs, which added to international tensions. Fort Screven was considered to be of particular strategic importance because it guarded one of the best ports, Savannah, on the east coast.

During the early 1900's, Fort Screven was commanded by a succession of Coast Artillery Corps officers, seldom above the rank of Captain. Officer assignments to the fort were usually of short duration and this sometimes caused a poor transition of command.

By late 1901 the post commander recognized that the fort was overcrowded. A second battery of troops

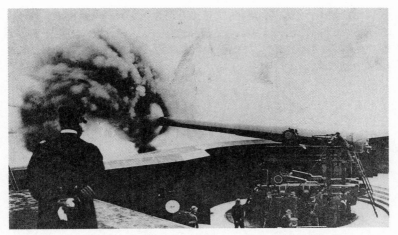

Battery Garland's 12-Inch Gun fired for practice.

had arrived the year before and about 300 of his troops were living in tents. He petitioned the War Department for: six additional officers quarters, a ward and a morgue for the post medical facility, a school house, a recreation room for the enlisted men and additional enlisted barracks that would include space for 25 or 30 members of a proposed band. Despite the efforts of many post commanders. however, there was never a military band stationed permanently at Fort Screven. Fort Screven hosted a drum and bugle corps from 1928 to 1940. The post commander asked also for improvements to the parade ground and the installation of searchlights. He received very little from this "wish list".

In 1900 it was determined that Fort Screven had grown to the size that it needed its own post office. The Savannah Beach post office, which had been located at Fort Screven, was moved to the south end of the island near a resort hotel built by the Central of Georgia railroad. This location was also near the end of the railroad tracks. The new Fort Screven post office was housed in the Martello Tower, which also served as the residence of Alice F. Evans, the first postmistress.

Tybee Hotel and Railroad Tracks, 1923

Living in the Martello Tower was apparently disconcerting for Mrs. Evans at times. Early on the mornings when the Fort Screven guns were fired for target practice, the resulting vibrations caused objects to be shaken off tables, shelves, and the mantelpiece. The officers finally began to warn Mrs. Evans in advance of a practice firing, so that she could take precautions to protect her belongings.

During the early years of the 1900's, sports and other types of recreational programs were organized for soldiers stationed at the fort. In the summer of 1900, a Fort Screven baseball team was organized. It competed against teams on Tybee Island and in Savannah. The soldiers also organized and participated in boxing matches and shooting competitions.

The post's first Christmas party was held on Christmas Eve in 1900. Elizabeth and Sue Schench, daughters of the post commander, planned and organized the event. All Tybee Island children, as well as the children of Fort Screven military personnel and local fishermen, were invited to attend the event held in the new officer's quarters.

Historical records reveal that, for the most part, the relationship between the Fort Screven soldiers and the citizens of Tybee was one of respect and cooperation. It is an interesting fact that during the fort's early years, a few of the soldiers served as island policemen and wore badges both on and off duty. At times, the city of Savannah Beach depended on Fort Screven for other services, such as electricity, water, fire protection, etc.

Plans were made in August of 1900 to establish some sort of recreation room for the enlisted men. A branch of the Army and Navy Young Men's Christian Association volunteered to set up such a facility on the post. The recreation room would contain reading material furnished by the Helen Gould Circuit Library, a wide selection of games, and the services of an organ.

Even though there was still no chaplain assigned to the fort, the spiritual well-being of the soldiers was not overlooked. Clergymen from Savannah conducted religious services on a regular basis. The Reverend James Y. Fair, Pastor of the Independent Presbyterian Church, held services in the enlisted men's barracks in May 1901. Attendance at the meeting was described as poor. A newspaper story offered an explanation as to the reason for the disappointing turnout—"because the men had just been paid."

First Lieutenant Leroy S. Lyon, who served as a battery commander at Fort Screven in the latter part of 1900 and the early part of 1901, was the inventor of an electrical device for firing the types of guns at Fort Screven. He developed this device after he had been transferred to another post. Lyon received promotion to Captain and returned to Fort Screven as post commander on October 1, 1901.

In August, 1902, an editorial in the New York Herald stated that Fort Screven was "one of the forts with poor strength and efficiency." It stated further that the soldiers assigned to the post were "new to military work and using undependable guns." The post commander, Lieutenant Colonel O'Hara, disturbed by these remarks about his installation, replied, "If all forts are as efficient and dependable as Fort Screven, the alarm is needless."

The fort's facilities continued to expand. In 1902 the War Department purchased a part of Beacon Pond, a portion of the Farber tract, to expand the hospital area. In December of that year, an additional 62 acres to be used for a parade ground were also purchased by the War Department.

By early 1903 submarine warfare became a subject of concern to the United States. Of more specific concern was the submarine fleet being developed by Germany. Captain J. C. Gilmore, Jr. was ordered to Savannah to take charge of anti-submarine defense preparations off Tybee Island. The harbors of Savannah and Charleston, South Carolina were the first sites along the Atlantic Coast to be fortified against the submarine menace. Captain Gilmore established his headquarters at Fort Screven.

Major General Adna R. Chaffee, Commander, Department of the East, inspected Fort Screven in February 1903 and immediately ordered that defensive preparations be intensified and that long-range plans

Fort Screven's Baseball Team, 1916.

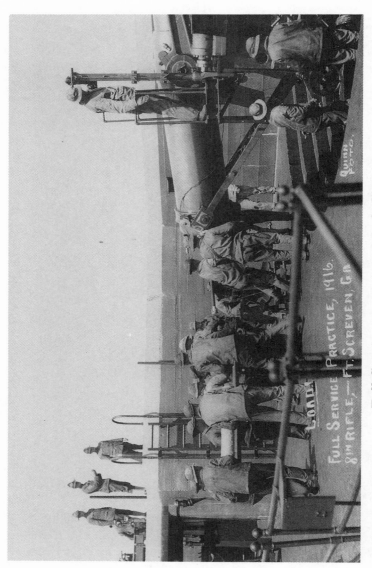

Full-Service practice on 8-Inch Gun.

for improvements in the installation be formulated. Within two months, the big guns were being fired every three months. Captain Gilmore took this as a cue to step up his anti-submarine defense activities. In the meantime, a mess hall and dance hall were added to the fort's facilities.

The United States Congress passed the Militia Act in 1903, thereby causing a reorganization of the Georgia Militia into the Georgia National Guard. This restructuring led to the organization of coast artillery national guard units which trained at Fort Screven each summer until the beginning of World War I.

Between 1906 and 1909 a battle commander's station, five other command stations, nine control stations and power plants were constructed. Searchlights were finally installed and ninety-two anti-submarine mines, with all accessories, were put into place.

There was a post elementary school established for the children of military and civilian personnel. After completing elementary school, the children attended high schools in Savannah, using the supply boat to get to and from school.

On March 19, 1913, a fire of undetermined origin gutted the old Martello Tower, destroying the Fort Screven post office and the living quarters of postmistress Alice Evans. The post office was reopened in another post building. When Evans retired, she was replaced by Mary O'Brien Lynch. A new post office building was eventually constructed and when Lynch retired, the position was filled by her daughter, Nell Lynch Devine. Unfortunately, the historic Martello Tower was blown up in 1914 because it obstructed the field of fire of one of the guns.

When World War I began in Europe in 1914, President Woodrow Wilson, desiring to keep the United States out of the war, issued a proclamation of neutrality. Disregarding this neutrality, German agents conducted a campaign of subversive activities designed to hinder American shipping of material to the Allies in Europe. German submarines expanded their operations in the Atlantic Ocean.

In the Summer of 1914, Fort Screven's soldiers frequented McFadden's Dance Hall at Savannah Beach, played baseball and read in the Savannah Morning News about a proposed road, to be built by convict labor, that would run from Savannah to Tybee Island. Troops of the 14th Coast Artillery kept the fort's guns in readiness, and conducted land and sea patrols to guard against submarine incursions and subversive activities.

Germany announced to the world on January 31, 1917 that it would henceforth engage in "unrestricted submarine warfare." This turn of events voided the United States' position of neutrality and Congress declared war against Germany on April 6, 1917.

German submarine activity increased in the Atlantic Ocean during World War I, but the action was minimal along the South Carolina and Georgia coasts. Thus, in yet another war, Fort Screven's powerful guns were fired only for practice. Battery Brumby's four 8-inch guns and Battery Habersham's 12-inch rifled mortars were dismantled and shipped to France to be used in the war against Germany.

❧ 4 ☙

Arrival Of
The 8th Infantry Regiment

World War I was often referred to, by the optimists of the world, as "the war to end all wars." Therefore, when the Armistice was signed, the United States government felt that there was no longer a need for a large military establishment. In May 1921, Fort Screven was assigned a new commanding officer, Lieutenant Colonel H. K. Taylor. In less than three months, the War Department announced that the installation would be inactivated. Two officers and fewer than thirty troops would remain at the post as caretakers. Some Fort Screven officers expressed to the media their reluctance to leave the small Georgia post. "We have become in love with this beautiful spot on the Atlantic, and it will be with sincere regret that we leave it," they said.

The inactivation of Fort Screven proceeded as scheduled. All of the big guns, with the exception of three, were dismantled and removed from the fortifications. The caretaker detachment remained at the fort for less than a year. During the summer of 1921 the post was used as a training site for members of the Citizens Military Training Camp (CMTC) from Georgia, South Carolina and Florida. Among units receiving training during this time was the 325th Infantry (Reserve).

39

In early 1922 several Savannah civic organizations asked the War Department for permission to use the Fort Screven buildings for some of their activities. The War Department replied that it was reconsidering the fort's closure and that it might assign some of the troops then on occupation duty in Germany to the post on their return to the United States.

Fort Screven was saved from inactivation when in April 1922, the War Department announced that a part of the Eighth Infantry Regiment would be assigned to the fort, "in the near future." City officials immediately started making plans to give the troops what the newspaper called a "hilarious welcome."

The Eighth Infantry Regiment, under the command of Colonel William T. Bates, arrived at the Port of Savannah aboard the United States transport *St. Mihiel* on February 7, 1923. The regiment had served

German War Brides of 8th Infantry (Sav. News).

Citizens Military Training Camp units (CMTC) were trained at Fort Screven

with the occupation forces in Germany from July, 1919 to January 1923. Some of the men were accompanied by their German wives and babies. They were the last American troops to return from Europe after World War I.

The regiment was treated to a gala welcoming by the citizens of Savannah and by many local and national dignitaries. Their arrival was announced by the ringing of the city's bells and the firing of a salute by the historic Washington Guns of the Chatham Artillery. There were parades, celebrations, speeches and a reception and ball for the officers and their wives at the DeSoto Hotel. The well-known newspaper publisher of the day, William Randolph Hearst, sent his private train to transport the First Battalion to its new home at Fort Screven and the remainder of the regiment, including regimental headquarters, to its new station at Fort Moultrie, South Carolina.

Prior to its assignment to Fort Screven, the Eighth Infantry Regiment already had a long history and had distinguished itself on the field of battle in all American military encounters up through World War I. It would be the regiment's destiny later to carry on this distinguished service through World War II, Korea and Viet Nam.

Organized by Act of Congress on July 5, 1838, the Eighth Infantry Regiment was stationed at Madison Barracks, New York. The regiment later moved to the Wisconsin Territory where it participated in operations against the Winnebago Indians. When hostilities ended and negotiations for the resettling of the Indians had been completed, The Eighth served for a brief period at Jefferson Barracks, Missouri. It moved from there to Florida for a four-year campaign against the Seminole Indians.

In the Fall of 1845, war with Mexico was imminent. The regiment became a part of Brevet Brigadier General Zachary Taylor's "Army of Occupation" in Texas. Serving under Taylor's command, the unit fought in the battle of Palo Alto, the first combat for the entire regiment as a unit, then again in the battle of Resaca de la Palma. Later, in a driving rain, the regiment scaled the heights at Monterey, surprising the enemy and capturing the city and the bishop's palace.

The following year Taylor's forces moved south and joined General Winfield Scott's expeditionary force in an amphibious assault that captured the city of Vera Cruz. They engaged the Mexican army at Cerro Gordo and Cherubusco, and then, after failed peace negotiations, subdued the enemy at Molino del Rey and Chapultepec, in rapid succession. The Eighth then took part in the capture of Mexico City on September 14, 1845.

In the years immediately prior to the Civil War, elements of the regiment were distributed among forts and camps in Texas. Their duty was to again campaign against the Indians.

When the Civil War began, the regiment attempted to withdraw from Texas by way of the coast. During this movement, the regiment was captured by the military forces of the newly-organized Confederate States of America. Some members of the regiment became prisoners of war and others were paroled, that is, released after making a pledge that they would not fight against the Confederacy.

At the time of the regiment's capture, Corporal John C. Hesse of Company A, and Sergeant-Major Joseph K. Wilson concealed the regimental colors under their clothing and managed to carry them through Confederate lines, arriving safely in Washington D.C. on May 21, 1861. Not until October 1863 could a fair representation of the unit be assembled to conduct operations against the Confederacy.

During the Civil War, units of the reorganized Eighth Infantry Regiment participated in most of the major campaigns, to include Antietam, Chancellorsville, Gettysburg, the Atlanta Campaign, and others. The regiment was finally united at Baltimore, Maryland on August 31, 1865. During the period of Reconstruction, from 1866 to 1870, it was stationed in the Carolinas.

In April of 1898, the regiment moved to Chickamauga Park for training before it sailed in June of that year for Cuba. On June 22 it landed at Daiquiri as part of the V Corps. The regiment marched into Siboney without encountering opposition and later in the month was near Santiago, preparing for the attack on El Caney. The battle raged from morning until late afternoon when the Spanish attempted to escape to Santiago.

The regiment's duty station was Havana and Columbia Barracks until September 1899, when the 3rd Battalion was sent to Fort Snelling, Minnesota. The remainder of the regiment joined the 3rd Battalion in July 1900 and remained in Minnesota until orders sent two battalions to the Philippines for duty against the insurgents. The First Battalion remained in the United States to garrison posts in Minnesota, North Dakota and Montana. In 1902, the First Battalion was sent to Alaska to be joined by two more companies upon the return of the regiment from the Philippines.

Reunited two years later in New York, the regiment again sailed to the Philippines for a two-year tour of duty. It returned from Manila and landed in San

Francisco on April 15, 1908. In early 1912, the unit was sent to the Philippines for a third time, where it remained until the United States' entry into WW I,

The ship transporting the regiment from the Philippines to the United States was damaged in a severe typhoon and forced to go into dry dock at Nagasaki, Japan, for extensive repairs. The mishap delayed the regiment's arrival in San Francisco until late September 1917. This late return to the United States caused such a lengthy postponement of its departure for Europe that the Eighth Infantry Regiment reached Breast only two days before the Armistice.

After the war, the regiment moved to Coblenz, Germany for occupation duties. Companies D and M were the last units of the regiment to leave Germany and were therefore present at the lowering of the colors at Ehrenbreitsstein on January 24, 1923, before sailing to join the remainder of the regiment in the United States

❧ 5 ❧

Lt. Col. Marshall Takes Command

During the early years of the Eighth Infantry Regiment's assignment to Fort Screven, the installation was transformed from a coast artillery fortification to an infantry post. Completion of this task required repairs to existing facilities and the construction of new ones. This came at a time when the United States Army was being reduced to a mere shadow of its former World War I strength; Congress was cutting War Department appropriations to the bone.

Lieutenant Colonel Ralph C. Barton was assigned as battalion and post commander at Fort Screven in early 1928. He supervised the construction of barracks, dependent quarters, a post exchange and a commissary. The army used profits from post exchanges to build a gymnasium having a basketball court and a boxing arena. The building also served, among other uses, as a church, a dance hall and a theater for the showing of silent motion pictures.

Sound motion pictures had become a reality by late 1929. In 1930 a brick motion picture theater, equipped for sound, was constructed at Fort Screven. It was one of the earliest sound motion picture theaters in the Savannah area.

Company D Barracks and Mess Hall, 1936

Post Exchange and Grocery Store, 1936

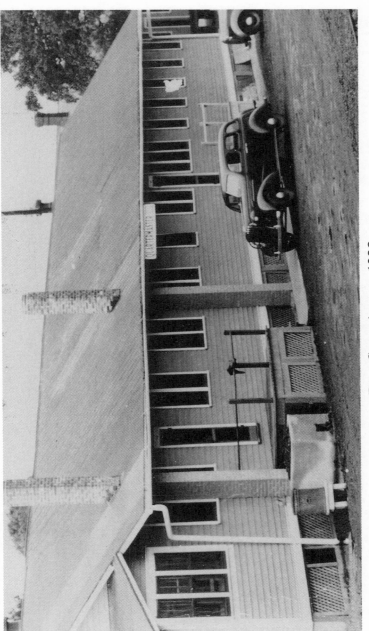

Post Commissary, 1936

Post Chapel and Gymnasium, 1936

Post Theater, built in 1930

The worst economic depression ever suffered by the United States began in 1930; it kept the country in its grip for ten years. During this bleak period in American history, it was Fort Screven's destiny to contribute to federal programs to get the country back on its economic feet. Fort Screven fulfilled its role during these trying days through the leadership of a new commander, Lieutenant Colonel George Catlett Marshall, a career soldier on whose shoulders the stars would one day fall.

Marshall came to Fort Screven in the spring of 1932 from duty with the Infantry School at Fort Benning, Georgia. He had turned down offers for more prestigious and higher paying assignments in the Philippines, and consideration for the Superintendency of the Virginia Military Institute. He was pleased to get the small Georgia post because he thought that, at that point in his military career, duty with troops was more desirable.

Lt. Col. George C. Marshall

Lieutenant Colonel Marshall's new command consisted of fewer than 400 men, but he accepted the assignment with cheerfulness, plunging into his new job with characteristic enthusiasm. "However small," he stated in a letter to his former commander and friend, General John "Blackjack" Pershing, "it at least keeps me away from office work and high theory."

In the early years of the twentieth century, members of the military services were shown very little respect by the American public. That attitude had prompted the United States Congress in 1910 to pass legislation making it illegal for public facilities to refuse service to military people. The civilian-military relationship in Savannah was better than average at the time of Marshall's arrival in 1932, but it was still not good. Determined to start off on the right foot in his new command, he immediately began laying the groundwork for friendship and cooperation between the Fort Screven soldiers and citizens of the local community.

Shortly after their arrival on post, Lieutenant Colonel Marshall and his wife, Katherine, attended Sunday worship services at Christ Episcopal Church in Savannah. Members of the congregation were amazed and pleased that the new Fort Screven commander had made an effort to pay his respects to the citizens of Savannah. He was introduced to several community leaders who were members of the church. On the following day, Savannah Mayor, Thomas Hoynes, returned the courtesy by visiting the Marshalls at Fort Screven. Soon thereafter, the mayor arranged for the delivery of several crepe myrtle plants to help beautify the post. Many of these crepe myrtles can still be seen surrounding Jaycee Park. Local mayors and other dignitaries were often invited to ceremonies at the fort. A new era of respect and cooperation began to evolve.

Lieutenant Colonel Marshall placed as much emphasis on military housekeeping as he did on military training. On his early morning horseback rides about the post, he made note of an area that needed landscaping or a garden that deserved commendation. One young officer wrote that Marshall oversaw his post "as would a southern planter his domain." There is a story that Marshall once observed two young ladies playing tennis while wearing dirty shoes. He ordered that henceforth their shoes would be whitened, so as to present a good example to his men. Marshall chose to lead more by example than by issuing orders. It was a foolish young officer who did not maintain his quarters and grounds to the accepted standard.

Marshall consistently concerned himself with the welfare of his men. With the help of a local civic organization, he purchased a confiscated rum runner and made the vessel available to soldiers and their families for picnics or fishing. Recognizing the tight economy and the resulting financial burdens on the soldiers under his command, he personally supervised the laying out of vegetable gardens and chicken yards on the post. He ordered the mess halls to prepare extra portions of food, put them in containers and sell them, at cost, to the lower ranking men with families.

Soon after Franklin D. Roosevelt was elected president in March 1933, he began to push his "New Deal" legislation. The new laws and programs were designed to alleviate the suffering of millions of jobless and hungry Americans, casualties of the "Great Depression".

One of the first relief programs favored by President Roosevelt and approved by Congress was the Civilian Conservation Corps (CCC). The program's purpose was to employ thousands of idle young men in reforestation and flood control projects, and to fight forest fires.

The United States Army got the job of setting up and running the CCC camps. The War Department notified corps commanders that the army must be prepared to organize and administer as many as one hundred thousand men. The prevailing assumption was that the army's task would be to enroll those selected for the program, transport them to army stations, and organize them into self-sustaining companies. Experts estimated that the process would take four weeks at most, after which the men would be assigned to work projects.

Fort Screven received notification that the army's IV Corps area, of which it was a part, had a quota of 7,100 trainees. Marshall was informed that the scheduled corps maneuvers were being canceled and that detachments already on their way to the maneuver area were to be recalled.

Federal directors of the program soon recognized that only the army was sufficiently equipped to organize and operate the camps. The army's original role expanded. On April 12, orders were issued giving the army charge of all CCC functions, with the exception of administration and technical supervision of the work projects.

Early in June 1933, Lieutenant Colonel Marshall was named commanding officer of District F of the IV Corps, with headquarters at Fort Screven. Marshall and his troops became responsible for establishing, organizing and supplying CCC camps throughout

Georgia and Florida. The first camp was established at Fort Screven. Other nearby camps were at Fort Pulaski and Hinesville. One important local project of the CCC was restoration work on Fort Pulaski, which had been neglected and had begun to deteriorate. Fort Pulaski is, at this writing, a national monument administered by the National Park Service.

Civilian Conservation Corps Camp 460.

Marshall found that the CCC program required most of his energy as well as most of the resources of his command at Fort Screven. When he was asked what he could spare for the CCC work he replied, "Leave my post surgeon, my commissary officer, my post exchange officer and my adjutant, and I will run this command with first sergeants." He eventually had to do just that.

During this time, the IV Corps headquarters decided to continue the Civilian Military Training Camp program, but the number of trainees was decreased, and training responsibilities were assigned to reserve officers.

From the beginning of the year, 1933, Marshall had

known that he was in line for promotion. Because of
the heavy workload of the CCC program, and because
his replacement had not arrived, Marshall requested
that his transfer to Eighth Infantry headquarters at
Fort Moultrie, South Carolina be delayed. The re-
quest was granted.

District F, IV Corps CCC Headquarters area, 1935

The Marshalls were given a farewell dinner in
Savannah on June 26 at which the president of the
Chamber of Commerce presented Lieutenant Colonel
Marshall with a field marshal's baton and dubbed
him the "Marshal of Savannah." Three days later, he
assumed command of the Eighth Infantry Regiment
and in July received his promotion to full colonel. He
was replaced at Fort Screven by Lieutenant Colonel
Clyde R. Abraham.

Colonel Marshall continued to work with the CCC
program during his tenure at Fort Moultrie. After
relinquishing his command of the Eighth Infantry
Regiment, he served in other assignments up to and
including World War II, in which his abilities as a

military leader were recognized with his selection as U. S. Army Chief of Staff. After his retirement from the army at the end of World War II, he continued to serve his country as Secretary of State and as Secretary of Defense. He was the architect of the "Marshall Plan" for the rebuilding of Western Europe after the devastation of World War II. Marshall was respected by the world as a man of peace as well as a military leader. This was proven when he was awarded the Nobel Peace Prize.

Even though George C. Marshall served at Fort Screven for but a short time, his contributions to, and influences on, the history of that military installation are legend.

❧ 6 ❧
The Fort Screven Soldier

During the depression years prior to World War II, soldiers stationed at Fort Screven followed a routine daily schedule. Reveille sounded at 5:45 a.m. and breakfast began 45 minutes later, by which time the soldier had showered, shaved, dressed, made his bed and cleaned his barracks area. He reported to his duty station at the 7:30 a.m. work call.

The training schedule for men of the Eighth Infantry Regiment's First Battalion included dismounted drill, bayonet and grenade instruction and marksmanship firing of the rifle, machine gun, automatic rifle, and pistol. There were constant classes in other military subjects. Army training manuals and field manuals served as texts. Combat training followed up the classes and drills.

Each day, members of Company D went to the post stables to groom and care for the company's mules. Company D was a machine gun company and the mules were used to transport the unit's weapons.

Each year the battalion traveled to Fort Benning, Georgia to take part in field maneuvers. This was the home of its parent organization, the Fourth Division, In addition to following the unit's training schedule, many of the soldiers worked at training several hundred Civilian Military Training Camp (CMTC) troops from Georgia and Florida one month, and army reserve officers the following month. Both groups of trainees were housed in the same tent area.

Post Stables, 1935

Lieutenant Colonel Jesse C. Drain became commander of First Battalion and the post in 1932. He was immediately faced with the military cutbacks resulting from the severe economic depression. That year, no funds were allocated for the purchase of ammunition for marksmanship training. Firing range instruction was deleted from the training schedule and not resumed until 1936.

In 1932 the federal government lowered the salaries of civil service employees by ten percent. The 1936 appropriations bill overturned these salary cuts and restored civil service pay to its previous level. The same legislation put a little more money in the pockets of the Fort Screven soldiers. It was not uncommon for a private to be appointed as an acting mess sergeant or CCC instructor. For this duty he was paid

$17.85 per month. The 1936 appropriations bill increased his pay to $19.95 per month.

Post Cmdr. Lt. Col. Jesse C. Drain and staff

Soldiers of the lowest ranks, not only at Fort Screven but throughout the United States Army, existed on credit from one payday to the next. They called this living on "jawbone," from the persuasive talk needed to secure credit or to borrow money from a buddy. Many obtained coupon books on credit and paid for them the following payday. With these coupons, they purchased toilet articles, tobacco and beer at the post exchange and attended movies at the post theater for ten cents a showing. If a soldier needed cold, hard cash he could usually find someone willing to buy his coupons, often at a steep discount. The Fort Screven soldiers could get credit at nearby civilian establishments where they could buy beer at ten cents a bottle or whiskey at ninety cents a quart. Again, payment was due the next payday.

Like all soldiers throughout history, the Fort Screven soldiers looked forward to getting a pass to go to town. They traveled between Fort Screven and Savannah by train until this service was discontinued on July 31, 1933. After the train stopped running, the men could travel by bus from Tybee to the terminal located at Wright Square in Savannah for a round-trip fare of thirty-five cents.

In downtown Savannah the soldiers had a choice of several good restaurants, movie theaters and night spots. For $2.00, a soldier could find female companionship at "Indian Lil's," which also sold beer and whiskey. One or two trips a month into Savannah was

Soldiers at the Post Exchange, 1905

1st Battalion, 8th Infantry Regiment Company A, 1936

1st Battalion, 8th Infantry Regiment Company B, 1936

1st Battalion, 8th Infantry Regiment Company C, 1936

1st Battalion, 8th Infantry Regiment Company D, 1936

Fort Screven Railroad Station

all that the average soldier could afford. Then it was back to the post and "jawbone" credit until payday.

The last bus of the day from Savannah to Fort Screven began its run at midnight. If a soldier missed this bus, he had to wait for the first scheduled departure the next morning, which would get him back to the post just in time for reveille. However, if one of the bridges on the new highway opened for river traffic, causing a delay in the bus's arrival, he would not make it to the post in time. The wrath of his first sergeant or company commander would descend on him when the did show up.

When the soldiers got off duty at the end of the day, unless they had special details, they often went to the beach for a swim. Some walked up the beach to the area of the Tybee Hotel, where they could perhaps meet lady visitors. These casual meetings often led to romance, and even marriage.

The army discouraged soldiers of lower rank from getting married. An often heard saying was, "If the army wanted you to have a wife, it would have issued you one." Ordinarily, only NCO's (Non-Commissioned Officers) were given official U. S. Army permission to marry and the "unofficial" wives of other soldiers were not recognized by the army and therefore did not enjoy post exchange, commissary, and other post privileges.

Frequent dances enlivened the Tybrisa Pier and Pavilion, Tybee's premier dance hall. When big bands performed, soldiers could purchase tickets at a special price of fifty cents each, with payment due the next payday. Soldiers who could not afford to pay the price of admission were apt to dance on the beach under the pavilion.

On such special evenings, the soldiers often pooled their money to buy moonshine. In the opinion of some aficionados, the best moonshine came from Daufuskie Island. However, Tybee Island could boast a still or two where moonshine went for $1.50 per gallon.

A welcome distraction from the Fort Screven soldier's daily routine had to be the beauty contests that were conducted at the Tybrisa pavilion. The first Miss Georgia beauty contest was held at the Tybrisa on the afternoon of July 26, 1926. The sponsor was the Savannah Water Carnival, an annual event between 1924 and 1928.

Thirty-six young ladies from Southeast Georgia took part in the first contest. The winner was Lera Dixon, Miss Pierce County, her prize being a trip to New York and the Philadelphia Sesquicentennial.

Since 1921, contestants in the Miss America pageants wore one-piece, form-fitting bathing suits. However, the first Miss Georgia contest in 1926 was more decorous. The contest rules stated, "This contest is open for every young lady in Georgia who is eighteen

Lera Dixon
Miss Georgia, 1926

years or more and unmarried. Any costume may be worn except bathing suits, which will not be permitted." Lera Dixon's costume was described by the Savannah Morning News as an "afternoon gown of lavender with a picture hat to match." After the contest, many of the contestants, including the new Miss Georgia, changed into bathing suits and cavorted in the surf as both still cameras and motion picture cameras captured the scene on film.

There was no talent competition; nor were there interviews with the contestants. They walked slowly in front of the judges to soft music played by Dewey Holme's Savannahians, a ten-piece orchestra. This first Miss Georgia contest was viewed by more than two thousand people.

Queen's Ball and Selection of Miss Georgia at

TYBRISA

under

FAMOUS CRYSTAL BALL

with

DEWEY HOLM'S SAVANNAHIANS
TEN PIECE ORCHESTRA

The Finest Sea Food
at
Tybrisa Restaurant

Most Modern Bath Houses on
the Coast

BEAUTIFUL BATHING SUITS   ~   ELABORATE NIGHT BATHING

Tybee's Largest Dance Pavilion

The next Miss Georgia beauty contest held at the Tybrisa pavilion took place in 1939. The winner was Mary Durrence of Glenville. She had been selected as the Tomato Festival Queen the year before.

Fifteen young ladies competed in the three-day event sponsored by the Tybee Island Chamber of Commerce. The judge's panel included Governor Eugene Talmadge and members of the Board of Governors of the Georgia Bar Association. Dean Hudson and his orchestra furnished the music for the event.

The year 1941 saw the last Miss Georgia pageant

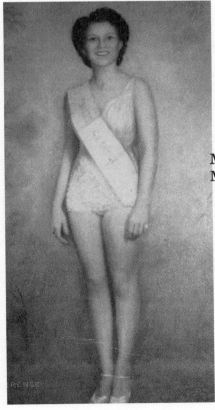

Mary Durrence
Miss Georgia, 1939

held at the Tybrisa pavilion. Jeanne Gillis of Soperton won that year's title. She competed in the Miss America pageant later that year.

Much of the soldier's off-duty time and energy was spent in sports activities. There were post boxing, basketball and baseball teams. Battalion champions were determined in annual tournaments. Fort Screven's First Battalion champions competed against the champions of the Second Battalion, stationed at Fort Moultrie, South Carolina, for the regimental championship. The post could boast of a squad of expert competitive riflemen that included the world's champion off-hand rifle shot, Sergeant Joseph Sharp of Company B, Eighth Infantry.

8th Infantry Regiment Baseball Team, 1934.

✖ 7 ✖

A New Mission—
The End Of An Era

When Lieutenant Colonel W. A. Ganoe became battalion and post commander in early 1937, he oversaw the dedication of a plaque to the honor of Brigadier General James Screven. Produced under the direction of Dr. M. L. Brittain of the Georgia School of Technology, the plaque occupied a spot in front of the guard house at the post's main gate.

A large crowd attended the unveiling ceremony on Saturday, November 7, 1937. Savannah Mayor Robert M. Hitch and Georgia Historical Commission member Thomas Gamble were among the dignitaries. Captain Ralph E. McCaskill, Fort Screven's Chaplain, gave the invocation. The Fort Screven Drum and Bugle Corps and the Savannah Police Band played musical selections. Richard M. Charlton, president of the Georgia Society, Sons of the Revolution, gave the principal address. Betty Lee Harris of Savannah and Anne Mallard Osterhout of Beaufort, South Carolina, both descendants of General Screven, unveiled the plaque. The plaque is now located in front of the former post gymnasium, which at this writing serves as the home of American Legion Post 154.

In June 1940, after seventeen years at Fort Screven,

Main Gate to Ft. Screven showing Memorial Plaque

the First Battalion, Eighth Infantry Regiment departed for Fort Benning, Georgia. After leaving Fort Screven, the regiment continued to build upon its proud combat record during World War II. In the Normandy invasion on June 6, 1944, the Eighth Infantry Regiment went ashore on Utah Beach under the command of Brigadier General Theodore Roosevelt, Jr. The regiment later served with the American forces in Korea and Viet Nam.

During its long and lustrous history, the Eighth Infantry Regiment earned forty-three campaign streamers to be displayed on its regimental colors, along with three Presidential Unit Citations. The unit has had seven medal of honor winners. Other famous commanders of the regiment, besides George C. Marshall, were Raymond O. Barton and James A. Van Fleet.

The month that the Eighth Infantry Regiment departed, 401 men and 107 vehicles of the Second Battalion, 70th Coast Artillery, under the command of Lieutenant Colonel Bird S. DuBois, garrisoned Fort Screven. The unit came to Fort Screven from Fort Monroe, Virginia.

In late September 1940, the 252nd Coast Artillery, North Carolina National Guard arrived at Fort Screven for training. They brought six of the unit's guns to Savannah by rail. Tractors towed the guns from Savannah to the fort. Bridges along the Tybee road had to be strengthened to accommodate the weight. Lieutenant Colonel DuBois supervised the training of the national guardsmen.

By the end of 1940 all of the national guard troops had left Fort Screven and the Second Battalion, 70th Coast Artillery had departed for its new station at recently-opened Camp Stewart at Hinesville, Georgia. Fort Screven got both a new commander, Colonel Charles B. Meyer, and a new mission. During the years of World War II, the fort became a diving school to train engineer troops for underwater salvage and the repair of bomb-damaged ports. The United States Army Engineer Diving and Salvage School at Fort Screven became the only school of its type operated by the army in the United States.

Colonel Meyer helped organize and train Port Construction and Repair Groups at Fort Screven. Members of these units were hand-picked engineers, riggers, divers, welders, mechanics, equipment operators, carpenters, clerks and cooks. Most of the men did this type of work in their civilian occupations. Because of their mission in the war, some people referred to them as "sailjers".

Engineer units that trained at Fort Screven during

Entrance to U.S. Army Diving and Salvage School.
(Sidney W. Falkenthal & Tybee Historical Society)

this era were the 1051st,1052nd, 1053rd and 1054th
Engineer Port Construction and Repair Groups. As a
part of their training, the engineer troops worked on
construction projects for the fort and the community.
The 1051st began to build a new post exchange restaurant in 1943 but could not finish the project because of pressing military duties. The 1052nd completed the project, using material salvaged from old
buildings. During maneuvers, the 1053rd constructed
a bridge and 500 feet of highway in the Camp Stewart
area, near Hinesville, in less than five days. The
1054th constructed a municipal dock for the town of
Savannah Beach.

Each repair group's training at Fort Screven's diving and salvage school lasted twelve intensive weeks.
Applicants had to pass exacting physical tests and
could be rejected for minor problems, a touch of

sinusitis for example, that did not bar a soldier from other assignments. The training required the student to work under water for extended periods, under trying conditions.

Manufacturers of the diving suit used a special type of rubber. As the diver descended into his underwater work environment, he opened a valve that admitted air into the suit until the air pressure within the suit was equal to that of the water outside. Over his G. I. shoes, the diver wore a pair of 35 pound rubber overshoes. A diving belt that resembled a soldier's cartridge belt added 83 pounds to the diver's weight. His metal diving helmet weighed 31 1/2 pounds and contained miniature glass portholes with protective brass grill covering.

In his diving suit, the diver had a telephone connection that kept him in constant communication with his companions on the surface. An electric amplifier made his voice audible to the entire crew of the dive tender.

It was estimated that the cost of the equipment needed to keep a diver on the job was approximately $7,000.

The average depth to which divers could descend and work with ease was approximately 90 feet. Beyond that depth, the pressure of the water was too great.

It became obvious in late December 1942 that Fort Screven's days as a military installation were numbered. The Fourth Service Command removed the three remaining guns and shipped them to a scrap metal collection point to be melted down for use in the war effort. The empty gun emplacements were all that remained of a once viable and formidable coastal fortification.

Colonel Meyer remained at the fort until the end of

U.S. Army
Diver's Suit
(Sidney W.
Falkenthal &
Tybee Historical
Society)

1943, organizing and training underwater salvage
and port construction groups for service in the European and Pacific theaters of operations. Colonel R. E.
Carmody replaced Colonel Meyer as post commander
and continued this training mission until there was
no longer any need for it.

At the end of August, 1944, the United States War
Department announced that Fort Screven was among
several military installations that the federal government declared surplus due to troops going overseas
and leaving the posts empty. Plans were to turn over
surplus installations to the Federal Housing Author-
ity for disposal. The federal government scheduled
Fort Screven's inactivation and placement on standby
status for October 21, 1944.

Discussions between city, county and state officials suggested possible uses for the Fort Screven property; these included a training facility for the state's national guard, a military preparatory school, or a state park. After much discussion about the fate of the fort, the state of Georgia finally notified the city that it was not interested in acquiring the property.

On November 27, 1945 the federal government sold Fort Screven to the town of Savannah Beach for $200,000. Included in the sale were the abandoned gun emplacements, land, buildings and four ocean-front lots that had been used as range finding stations.

In January 1946, the town of Savannah Beach offered all Fort Screven property at a public sale. The mayor and aldermen agreed that it would be in the municipality's best interest to sell the property as a whole. 134.37 acres of land and 265 buildings went on the auction block. On the morning of January 29, 1946, at Savannah Beach City Hall, Clerk of Council Henry M. Buckley opened the bids. The only bidder was Robinson Realty Company, agents for the Fort Screven Development Company. Dr. William A. Wexler purchased the four ocean-front lots for a high bid of $26,001.

The federal government retained possession and control of the Tybee Lighthouse and Coast Guard station. The city exempted from the sale the fire station, gymnasium, telephone exchange, post exchange, sewer and water pumps, crane building and shop, automobile workshop, garage, lubricating rack, and the wire fence that surrounded the reservation.

Thus Fort Screven ceased to be a military installation. Tybee Island's military heritage is kept alive in historical archives and in the memories of those who witnessed it.

❧ Epilogue ❧

Remembrances

Each year, thousands of tourists visit Tybee Island to enjoy its beautiful beaches and its hospitality. The island's other major attraction is its historic lighthouse, one of the few remaining working lighthouses open to the public. Many visitors to the lighthouse complex become aware of another chapter in Tybee Island's past only when they view the remains of the concrete and granite batteries that are focal points of remembrances of another time in the history of the nation and of Tybee Island.

When developers, and eventually individuals, bought the Fort Screven property, they gave little thought to the fact that the area might someday be eligible for designation as a national historic site. Therefore, the early development of the area as a residential community proceeded under very little control. At the time of this writing, local citizens groups, continuing to build upon what has been done in past years, are working to reverse the trend. On May 28, 1982, the Fort Screven Neighborhood Association succeeded in having the entire Fort Screven area placed on the National Register of Historic Places.

Persons enjoying a drive or a walk around the lighthouse area will see many remnants of the one-time military post. Immediately in front of the lighthouse property are Batteries Garland and Brumby. Battery Garland houses the Tybee Museum, and, like the lighthouse, is overseen by the Tybee Island Historical Society. At the time of this writing, Battery Brumby serves as the foundation for the Tybee Lite Shrine Club and for private residences that have been constructed atop its walls. Gun position #3 of Battery Brumby is being restored by the Historical Society. The ruins of Batteries Backus, Gant, Habersham and Fenwick are also on private property and can be viewed by traveling down Taylor and Pulaski Streets.

Battery Garland (Tybee Museum)

Two of the fort's former entrances are marked with interpretive signs containing the insignia of the Coast Artillery and the Eighth Infantry Regiment. Each sign contains a plaque commemorating Fort Screven's selection as a national historic site.

The post's main gate is at the junction of Campbell

Gun position No. 3 of Battery Brumby.

Avenue and Van Horn Street. The large white frame building at the intersection is the old guardhouse. Soldiers assigned to serve guard duty throughout the post stayed in this building during their tours of duty. The building now serves as Tybee's Community Center and is used for activities such as square dances, wedding receptions, family reunions. and as a meeting place for island organizations.

"There would be two soldiers on patrol outside the guardhouse all the time," related retired Colonel Earl Eubanks, who served as ordinance officer at the fort from 1934 to 1941. "They would pace back and forth, 120 steps per minute. Of course, no one ever counted to make sure." Eubanks returned to Tybee as a permanent resident in 1961.   The old guardhouse sits on the edge of what was once the parade ground. The area is now a community park and baseball diamond and is called Jaycee Park. During the military years,

Guard Detail in front of the Guardhouse.

Officer's Row as seen from Post Headquarters, 1907

a tall, white flagpole marked the center of the parade ground. Flanking the flagpole were two salute guns that were fired twice a day, at reveille and retreat.

One of Eubanks favorite stories is about the time that some mischievous youngsters stuffed the barrel of one of the guns with baseballs, rocks, sticks, and other material. When the crew fired the gun, the flying debris broke several windows in the area. Many years later, Eubanks' own son admitted to being one of the youthful culprits.

Perched atop a ridge that overlooks the park is a row of elegant turn-of-the-century frame houses, their expansive porches facing the sea. The homes served as quarters for senior officers and their families and became known as Officers Row. The homes are now privately owned. The area in front of the homes served as a parade ground, polo field and rifle range.

Also positioned on the rim of the park and across Van Horn Street is the Savannah Beach Nursing Home. This was the general area of the post hospital complex.

Another access to the Fort Screven area is by way of 2nd Avenue, which enters Gate # 2. This entrance is recognizable by two pillars with "Fort Screven" etched into each capstone. The pillars are topped by round globes that are lighted at night. Upon entering the gate, one begins a journey down Van Horn Street, which meanders from one end of the fort to the other.

A short distance inside Gate #2 is a red brick structure that is the shell of the old post theater. The building is now privately owned and, at this writing, plans are for it to be converted to private residences. Many Tybee residents remember when it was showing first-run movies and hosting stage performances for the entertainment of both soldiers and civilians.

Entrance Gate No. 2

Continuing along Van Horn Street from Gate #2, the visitor will pass many of the facilities that have been mentioned here. A short distance past the park and Guardhouse/Community Center, Veterans Drive intersects with Van Horn Street. The most prominent building on this part of Veterans Drive is a large white building that once was the old post gymnasium. The building now serves as the home of American Legion Post 154.

In 1969 veterans of 1st Battalion, 8th Infantry Regiment organized the Fort Screven Association and began to hold annual reunions at Tybee. Some of the men travel long distances to meet in the old post gymnasium and reminisce about their lives and experiences as Fort Screven soldiers. At the 1989 reunion, the veterans were honored by the presence of one of their oldest and most prominent commanders, retired General James A. Van Fleet. The General died in 1992 at the age of 100.

Across Veterans Drive from the gymnasium stands a red brick building that was the post bakery. It provided all of the bread that the commissary sold to soldiers and their families. The building is now a private home.

Post Gymnasium (American Legion Post 154).

At the intersection of Veterans Drive and Van Horn, an abandoned walkway leads to stone steps that were once the entrance to the post exchange and restaurant. What had once been a somewhat opulent structure with a stage and a large dance floor is now a disintegrating concrete slab covered with weeds and wildflowers.

In following Van Horn Street toward its end, one will pass through a section that was the quartermaster or supply area of the post. The only remnants of this once bustling part of Fort Screven are warehouses and two identical brick gas stations. The post laundry was where the water tower now stands. An incinerator was located on the site now occupied by the Tybee Recreation Department's ceramics building.

Older Tybee residents love to tell stories about Fort Screven and the way it was in its heyday. They evoke visions of ranks of suntanned men dressed in starched khakis, highly-polished riding boots and Sam Browne belts. Henry Jackson, son of Tybee's last lighthouse keeper, holds fond memories of sitting on his porch and watching Lieutenant Colonel Marshall ride majestically around the post on a beautiful horse. He remembers Sergeant Spud Grace who, "Stood so straight that he often appeared to bend over backwards."

Nell Lynch Devine has witnessed Fort Screven's history from its beginning to the present. As of this writing, she makes her home in the Fort Screven train depot where she served as the last ticket agent. The unpaved road that runs parallel with part of Van Horn Street was once the railroad tracks that led to the Fort Screven depot.

In 1987 Colonel Earl Eubanks accompanied a Savannah News-Press reporter on a driving tour of the Fort Screven area. They observed a seemingly unplanned conglomeration of military buildings that either had been abandoned or converted to private residences, intermingled with more modern homes and condominiums.

"It doesn't remind you of a military installation at all now," Eubanks said with obvious regret. "But Fort Screven used to be as pretty as any park in Savannah."

Bibliographical Notes

The author used the following references to prepare the manuscript:

Prologue—"Tybee's Early History"

Notes, video scripts and other documents from the files of the Tybee Island Historical Society; 50 Meddin Drive, Tybee Island, Georgia, 31328.

Chapter I—"The War Between the States"

Durham, Roger S. "Savannah: Mr. Lincoln's Christmas Present." *Blue & Gray Magazine*, February 1991, pp. 8-13.

Andrews, W. H. *Footprints of a Regiment*. Annotated and with an Introduction by Richard M. McMurry. Atlanta: Longstreet Press, 1992, pp. 9-11.

Chapter V—"Lt. Col. Marshall Takes Command"

Pogue, Forrest C. *George C. Marshall: Education of a General*. With the editorial assistance of Gordon Harrison. New York: The Viking Press, 1963, pp. 271-278.

The author and compilers of this book made extensive use of Articles on Fort Screven published in the *Savannah News-press* between 1897 and 1994.

About the Author

James Mack Adams is a retired educator who makes his home in the Fort Screven area of Tybee Island, Georgia, where he works as a freelance writer and journalist. He feeds his love of history by serving on the Board of Directors of the Tybee Island Historical Society and as a member of the Tybee Island Historic Preservation Committee. He also works as a living history interpreter and Civil War reenactor. He is Associate Editor of the island's monthly newspaper, the Tybee News. Other writing credits include a textbook and professional articles.

To order additional copies of

**A HISTORY
OF
FORT SCREVEN
GEORGIA**

Contact

Tybee Island Historical Society
Post Office Box 366
Tybee Island, GA 31328